BASS CLARINET FINGERING CHARTS
Scales & Songs

ISBN: 978-1-969068-07-2
© 2026 The Martin Freres Company, Merimax, LLC
All Rights Reserved

Kimber Books

Thank you!

Thank you for choosing Bass Clarinet Fingering Charts, Scales & Songs. This book is designed for the B♭ Bass Clarinet and serves as a clear, dependable reference for beginners and developing players.

Inside, you'll find fingering charts, scales, and familiar songs arranged to make learning both visual and musical. We begin with basic tutorials and gradually introduce more advanced concepts. Once you have the fundamentals down, you can jump to any section you like, and there is no required order.

Some scales and songs are easy and approachable, while others reach beyond the beginner clarinet range and may take more time to master. This book is meant to grow with you, serving as both an introduction and a lasting reference as your skills expand.

Each song includes a QR code that links directly to its audio recording. Listening before you play helps you understand how the notes fit together and strengthens your sense of tone, rhythm, and musical phrasing.

We hope this book becomes a steady companion on your musical journey, one you can return to often whether you're playing your first notes or exploring new challenges.

Happy playing!

Martin Freres

the
MARTIN FRERES COMPANY
MartinFreres.net

Let's Begin

Learning to play the bass clarinet can feel tricky at first, especially when trying to figure out which fingers to use for the notes on the page. That's why this book has fingering charts right below each note. These charts make it much easier to focus on playing instead of guessing. Here's how to use them.

Understand the Fingering Chart
Each note comes with a fingering diagram that shows you exactly which keys to press.
  - Black circles mean press this key down.
  - White and Gray circles mean don't press this key.

The fingering chart shown here is used for all the scales and songs in this book. On the music staff, the names of the notes are written above the staff to help you know what to play. Under each note, you'll see a fingering diagram that shows you where to put your fingers on the clarinet. This makes it easier to match the notes to the proper finger positions.

**Notes to Play:
Letter above - Note below**

**Bass Clarinet
Fingering**

For each note, press only the keys that are solid black.

By using the fingering charts, you'll learn faster and have more fun playing, now!

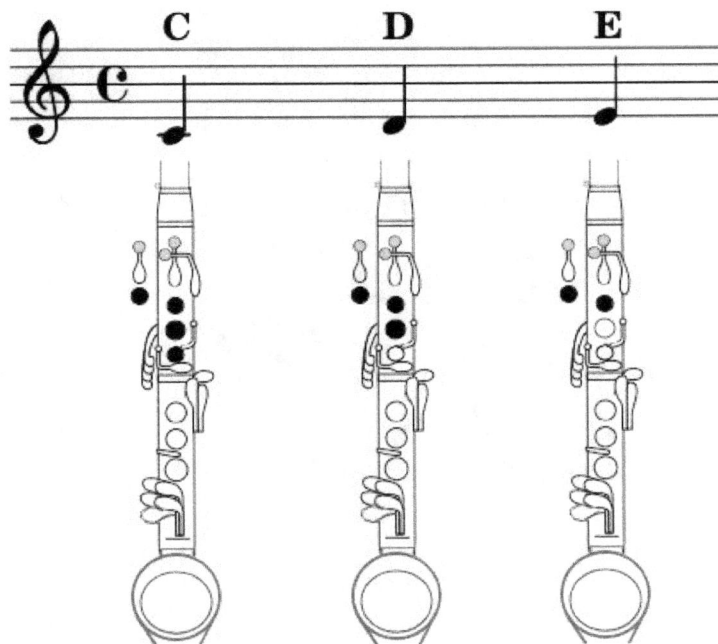

How to Use the QR Codes

Scan the QR code with your phone or tablet camera to hear the song. Listen and play what you hear. QR codes allow you to hear how the notes and rhythm sound together.

Scan the
QR Code

to Listen!

Bass Clarinet Fingering

Which Finger Goes Where?

1 = LH Index Finger
2 = LH Middle Finger
3 = LH Ring Finger
4 = RH Index Finger
5 = RH Middle Finger
6 = RH Ring Finger

R = Register Key
Th = Thumb Rest

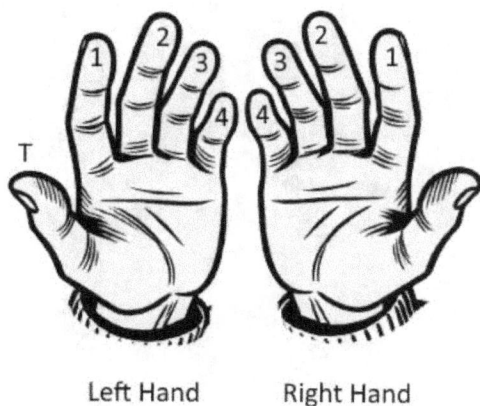

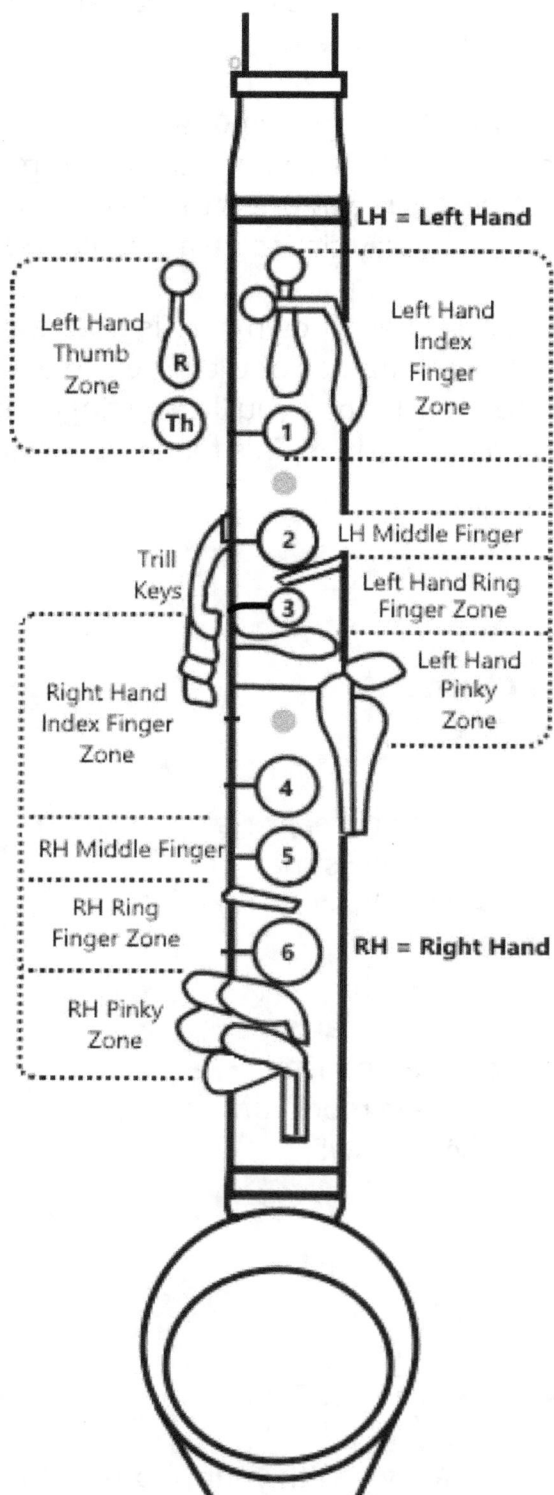

LH = Left Hand

Left Hand Thumb Zone

R

Th

Left Hand Index Finger Zone

1

LH Middle Finger

2

Trill Keys

Left Hand Ring Finger Zone

3

Left Hand Pinky Zone

Right Hand Index Finger Zone

4

RH Middle Finger

5

RH Ring Finger Zone

6

RH = Right Hand

RH Pinky Zone

Left Hand

Right Hand

TIP: Start with your left hand on top and your right hand on bottom. Your left-hand thumb supports the instrument and operates the back register key.

How to Hold the Bass Clarinet

1. Your Body Position

The bass clarinet is most often played seated, especially by students. Sit toward the front of the chair with both feet flat on the floor. Keep your back tall but relaxed, shoulders down, and chest open. Avoid leaning forward or slouching. The instrument should come to you naturally without forcing your head or body to move. If standing is required, use a neck strap or harness and maintain the same upright posture.

2. Instrument Support

The bass clarinet is supported by three main points:

- The neck strap or harness
- The right-hand thumb
- The mouthpiece at the embouchure

The instrument should feel balanced and secure without gripping or squeezing. Adjust the neck strap so the mouthpiece comes to your mouth easily when your head is level. You should not have to bend your neck down to reach the mouthpiece.

3. Mouth and Head Position

Bring the mouthpiece to your mouth, not your mouth to the mouthpiece. Keep your head upright and relaxed. The angle of the bass clarinet should allow the mouthpiece to enter the mouth comfortably without strain. The embouchure should be firm but flexible, with no excess pressure.

4. Left Hand and Fingers

- Place your left hand on the upper joint.
- Curve your fingers naturally over the holes and keys
- Keep fingers close to the keys at all times
- Avoid lifting fingers high off the instrument

The left-hand thumb rests behind the instrument and operates the register key as needed. Keep the thumb relaxed and ready, not tense.

5. Right Hand and Thumb

Place your right hand on the lower joint. Your right-hand thumb rests in the thumb rest or against the instrument for balance. It should support, not squeeze. The fingers should curve gently over the lower keys, staying relaxed and close to the instrument. If your hand feels strained, adjust the neck strap or instrument angle rather than gripping harder.

Learning to Play the Bass Clarinet

Making a Sound

Making a musical sound on the bass clarinet can take time and patience. Begin by practicing with just the mouthpiece and neck. Place the mouthpiece gently into the center of your mouth and form a firm but relaxed embouchure (mouth and lip position). Let the bottom lip rest lightly over the teeth and seal the corners of the mouth. Keep the chin flat and the throat open, as if quietly saying 'who.'

Start the air and use steady, supported breath. Do not bite or force the sound. Once you can produce a clear, steady tone on the mouthpiece and neck, assemble the full instrument and keep the same embouchure and air support. Adjust the angle of the instrument slightly if needed, but avoid moving the mouth. With consistent practice, the sound will become fuller, steadier, and more reliable.

Use the Charts While Learning Scales & Songs

When you start playing Scales & Songs, keep using the fingering charts as a guide. Play one note at a time and check your fingers if you need to. After a while, your fingers will begin to remember where to go, and you can follow the music sheet instead of the fingering charts.

Listen for Accuracy

Even if your fingers are in the right spots, your sound might still not be quite right if your breath control or lip positioning isn't right. Use the charts to make sure your fingers are correct, but also focus on creating a clear, steady sound for each note.

Move Away from the Charts

As you get better, challenge yourself to play scales and songs by looking only at the notes on the staff. Let your fingers do the work from memory. The more you practice this way, the more confident and independent you'll become.

By practicing with these charts and gradually using them less, you'll build strong skills faster and with less frustration. Always remember, the goal is not just to play notes, it's to make music. With time and effort, you'll be playing with confidence and having fun.

Starter C Major Scale

This is the starter C major scale beginning with the low note A rather than beginning with C. This allows new players to learn the notes of the C major scale before reaching for higher notes that can be tricky to learn. For this version, the notes are: A, B, C, D, E, F, G, then back to A.

For beginners, playing full scales can take time. Some of the lowest and highest notes need more practice, and that is perfectly fine. Play the notes you can, learn them at your own pace, and grow into the rest as you continue.

Each note comes with a fingering diagram showing you which keys to press.
- Black circles mean press this key down.
- White and Gray circles mean don't press this key.

Scan the QR Code

to Listen to the scale!

C Major Scale (Up)

Practicing the C major scale helps train your ear to hear the sound of a major key, which is important for playing songs and understanding how music fits together. We call it "Up" because the scale begins on the lower C note and moves higher with each new note. This scale is also known as the **C major scale ascending**, and it uses the notes C, D, E, F, G, A, and B. You will find these notes in many of the songs in this book.

For beginners, playing full scales can take time. The lower notes need more air, not tighter embouchure. And they need more practice too, and that is perfectly fine. Play the notes you can, learn them at your own pace, and grow into the rest as you continue.

Each note comes with a fingering diagram showing you which keys to press.
- Black circles mean press this key down.
- White and Gray circles mean don't press this key.

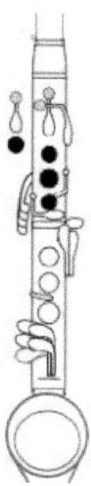

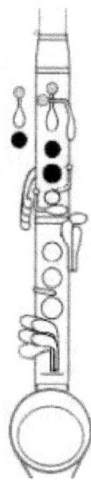

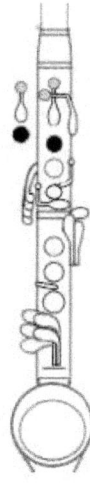

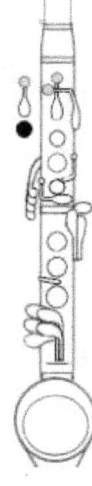

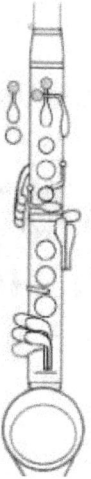

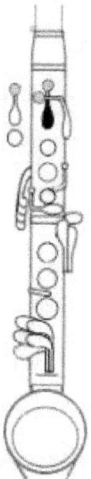

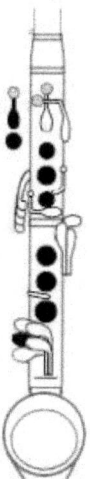

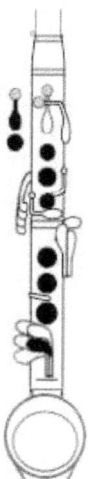

Scan the
QR Code

to Listen to
the scale!

C Major Scale (Down)

Here is the C major scale going down. We call it "Down" because the scale begins on the higher C note and every new note goes lower in sound. This is also known as the **C major scale descending** and we will play the notes C, B, A, G, F, E, D, then back to C, only lower.

For beginners, playing full scales can take time. For many players, descending scales feel different than ascending scales. The lower notes need steady air support and a relaxed embouchure to speak clearly. Take your time and focus on keeping the sound full and even as you move downward. Play the notes you can, learn them at your own pace.

Remember, each note comes with a fingering diagram showing you which keys to press.
   - Black circles mean press this key down.
   - White and Gray circles mean don't press this key.

C   B   A   G

F   E   D   C

Scan the QR Code

to Listen to the scale!

G Major Scale (Up)

This is the G major scale ascending. The scale begins on the G note and moves higher in sound with each new note. The G major scale includes the notes G, A, B, C, D, E, and F# (F sharp). The word **sharp** means the note sounds slightly higher in pitch than the regular note, in this case F.

For beginners, playing full scales can take time. The lower notes need more air, not tighter embouchure. And they need more practice too, and that is perfectly fine. Play the notes you can, learn them at your own pace, and grow into the rest as you continue.

Remember, each note comes with a fingering diagram showing you which keys to press.
- Black circles mean press this key down.
- White and Gray circles mean don't press this key.

Scan the QR Code

to Listen to the scale!

G Major Scale (Down)

Here is the G major scale descending. The scale begins on the higher G note and every new note goes lower in sound. For the G major scale descending we will play the notes G, F#, E, D, C, B, A, then back to G, only lower.

For beginners, playing full scales can take time. For many players, descending scales feel different than ascending scales. The lower notes need steady air support and a relaxed embouchure to speak clearly. Take your time and focus on keeping the sound full and even as you move downward. Play the notes you can, learn them at your own pace.

Remember, each note comes with a fingering diagram showing you which keys to press.
- Black circles mean press this key down.
- White and Gray circles mean don't press this key.

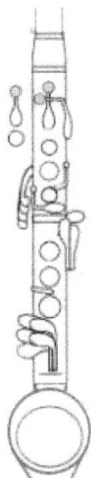

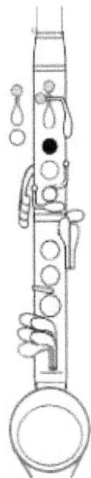

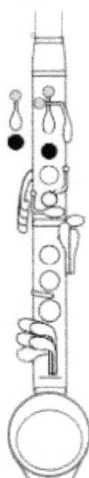

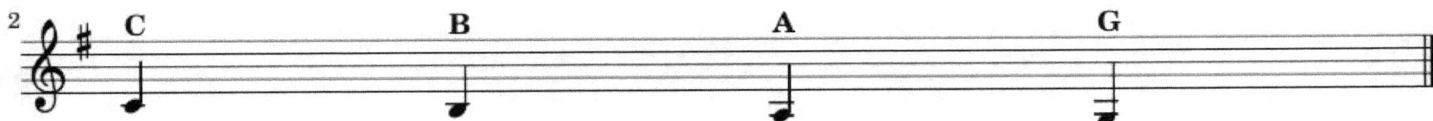

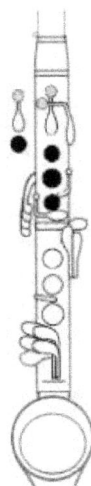

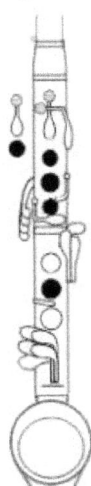

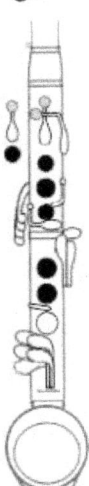

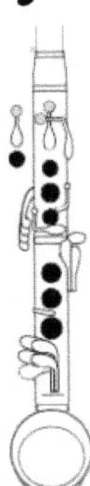

Scan the QR Code

to Listen to the scale!

F Major Scale (Up)

This is the F major scale ascending. The scale begins on the F note and moves higher in sound with each new note. The F major scale includes the notes F, G, A, B♭ (B flat), C, D, and E. The word **flat** means the note sounds slightly lower in pitch than the regular note, in this case B.

For beginners, playing full scales can take time. The lower notes need more air, not tighter embouchure. And they need more practice too, and that is perfectly fine. Play the notes you can, learn them at your own pace, and grow into the rest as you continue.

Remember, each note comes with a fingering diagram showing you which keys to press.
   - Black circles mean press this key down.
   - White and Gray circles mean don't press this key.

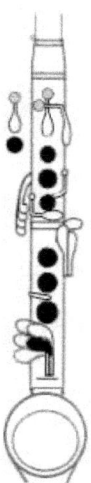

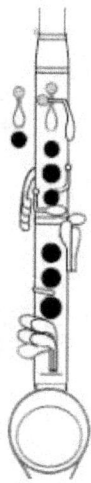

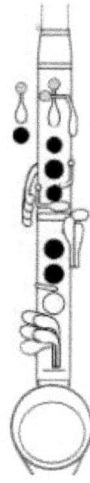

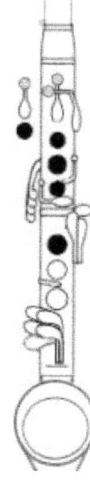

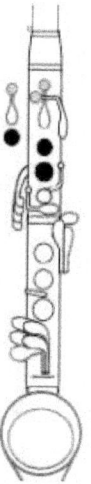

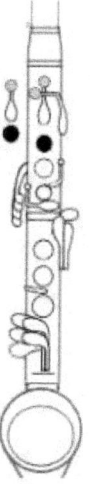

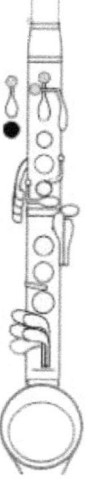

Scan the QR Code

to Listen to the scale!

F Major Scale (Down)

Here is the F major scale descending. The scale begins on the higher F note and every new note goes lower in sound. For the F major scale descending we will play the notes F, E, D, C, B♭, A, G, then back to F, only lower.

For beginners, playing full scales can take time. For many players, descending scales feel different than ascending scales. The lower notes need steady air support and a relaxed embouchure to speak clearly. Take your time and focus on keeping the sound full and even as you move downward. Play the notes you can, learn them at your own pace.

Remember, each note comes with a fingering diagram showing you which keys to press.
- Black circles mean press this key down.
- White and Gray circles mean don't press this key.

Scan the QR Code

to Listen to the scale!

D Major Scale (Up)

This is the D major scale ascending. The scale begins on the D note and moves higher in sound with each new note. The D major scale includes the notes D, E, F#, G, A, B, and C#.

For beginners, playing higher notes can take time. The upper notes need faster, focused air and steady embouchure support, not added pressure or biting. Keep the throat open and the air moving freely as you ascend. Play the notes you can at your own pace, and let the upper range develop gradually as you continue.

Remember, each note comes with a fingering diagram showing you which keys to press.
- Black circles mean press this key down.
- White and Gray circles mean don't press this key.

Scan the
QR Code

to Listen to
the scale!

D Major Scale (Down)

Here is the D major scale descending. The scale begins on the higher D note and every new note goes lower in sound. For the D major scale descending we will play the notes D, C#, B, A, G, F#, E, then back to D, only lower.

For beginners, playing higher notes can take time. The upper notes need faster, focused air and steady embouchure support, not added pressure or biting. Keep the throat open and the air moving freely as you descend. Play the notes you can at your own pace, and let the upper range develop gradually as you continue.

Remember, each note comes with a fingering diagram showing you which keys to press.
- Black circles mean press this key down.
- White and Gray circles mean don't press this key.

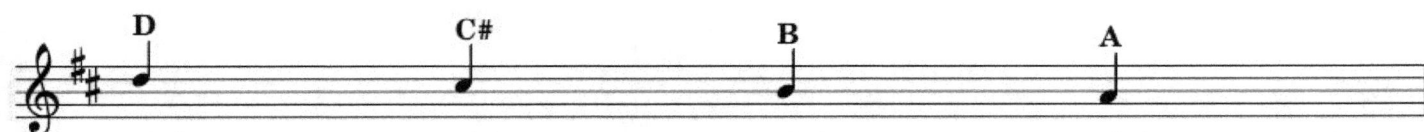

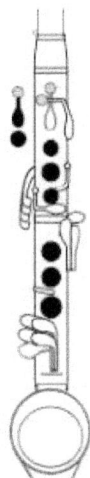

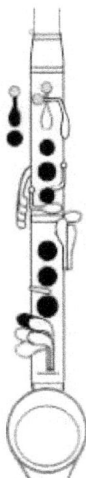

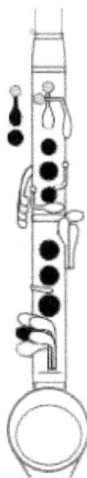

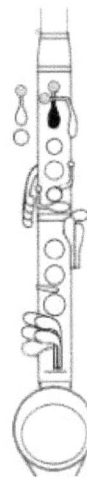

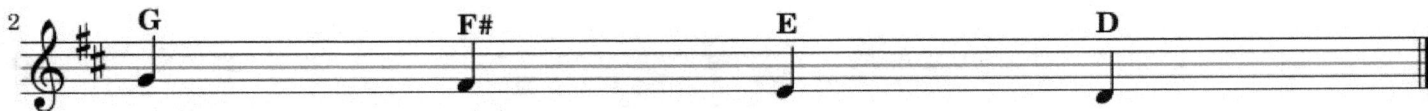

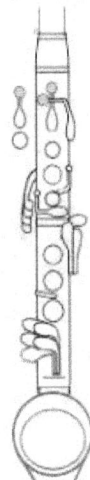

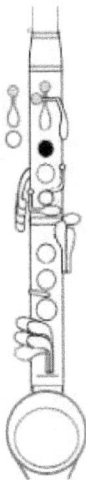

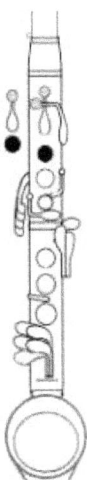

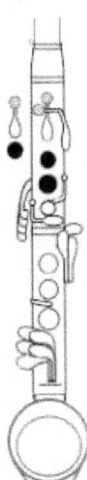

Scan the QR Code

to Listen to the scale!

Bb Major Scale (Up)

This is the Bb major scale ascending. The scale begins on the Bb note and moves higher in sound with each new note. The Bb major scale includes the notes Bb, C, D, Eb, F, G, and A.

For beginners, playing full scales can take time. The lower notes need more air, not tighter embouchure. And they need more practice too, and that is perfectly fine. Play the notes you can, learn them at your own pace, and grow into the rest as you continue.

Remember, each note comes with a fingering diagram showing you which keys to press.
- Black circles mean press this key down.
- White and Gray circles mean don't press this key.

Scan the QR Code

to Listen to the scale!

B♭ Major Scale (Down)

Here is the B♭ major scale descending. The scale begins on the higher B♭ note and every new note goes lower in sound. For the B♭ major scale descending we will play the notes B♭, A, G, F, E♭, D, C, then back to B♭, only lower.

For beginners, playing full scales can take time. For many players, descending scales feel different than ascending scales. The lower notes need steady air support and a relaxed embouchure to speak clearly. Take your time and focus on keeping the sound full and even as you move downward. Play the notes you can, learn them at your own pace.

Remember, each note comes with a fingering diagram showing you which keys to press.
   - Black circles mean press this key down.
   - White and Gray circles mean don't press this key.

Scan the
QR Code

to Listen to
the scale!

E♭ Major Scale (Up)

This is the E♭ major scale ascending. The scale begins on the E♭ note and moves higher in sound with each new note. The E♭ major scale includes the notes E♭, F, G, A♭, B♭, C, and D.

For beginners, playing higher notes can take time. The upper notes need faster, focused air and steady embouchure support, not added pressure or biting. Keep the throat open and the air moving freely as you ascend. Play the notes you can at your own pace, and let the upper range develop gradually as you continue.

Remember, each note comes with a fingering diagram showing you which keys to press.
   - Black circles mean press this key down.
   - White and Gray circles mean don't press this key.

Scan the QR Code

to Listen to the scale!

E♭ Major Scale (Down)

Here is the E♭ major scale descending. The scale begins on the higher E♭ note and every new note goes lower in sound. For the E♭ major scale descending we will play the notes E♭, D, C, B♭, A♭, G, F, then back to E♭, only lower.

For beginners, playing higher notes can take time. The upper notes need faster, focused air and steady embouchure support, not added pressure or biting. Keep the throat open and the air moving freely as you descend. Play the notes you can at your own pace, and let the upper range develop gradually as you continue.

Remember, each note comes with a fingering diagram showing you which keys to press.
- Black circles mean press this key down.
- White and Gray circles mean don't press this key.

Scan the QR Code

to Listen to the scale!

What is Your Embouchure?

em·bou·chure | \ ,äm-bü-'shủr

The embouchure is how a musician shapes and positions their lips, mouth, and facial muscles to control the sound and tone of a wind instrument, such as a bass clarinet. It is a delicate balance of muscle coordination and pressure that transforms air into music, acting as the "control panel" for sound quality, pitch, and projection on a wind instrument.

Your embouchure is how you use your lips, teeth, and mouth to play the clarinet, and it makes a big difference in how you sound. Let's talk about how to balance the pressure you use so your playing feels easier and your sound improves.

What Is Embouchure Pressure?
Think of your reed, lips, and teeth as a team working together to make music. If one part isn't doing its job, or if it's working too hard, it can mess things up.

Too much pressure: Your sound might become thin or squeaky.
Too little pressure: The sound could get airy or weak.

The goal is to find just the right amount of pressure so your reed vibrates freely, and you can produce a steady, warm tone.

How do you know if something's not quite right? Listen to your sound.

Squeaks: Your reed might not be vibrating evenly because of uneven pressure.
Breathy sound: This happens if your lips aren't sealing well around the mouthpiece.
Tired mouth muscles: You might be pressing too hard or using muscles that don't need to work as much.

Tips to Improve Your Embouchure

Bottom Lip: Roll it over your teeth to cushion the reed. No biting.

Top Teeth: Rest them lightly on the mouthpiece for stability.

Lip Shape: Form an "O" around the mouthpiece for a focused, airtight seal.

Notes, Beats & How to Count Them

Here's a quick guide to the most common note types and how long each one lasts. In this book, we focus on learning to play by listening to the piece and then playing what you hear. You'll learn more about timing as you continue your musical journey.

Eighth (8th) notes
Each eighth note lasts for half a beat. Use steady air and move quickly to the next note.

When we see a plus sign: + we say 'and'

Quarter notes
A quarter note lasts 1 full beat. Use steady air and hold each note for one full beat. Each beat lasts the same amount of time.

Half notes
We play each half note for a count of 2 beats. Use steady air and hold each note for a full 2 beats. Each note lasts the same amount of time.

Whole notes
We count each whole note for 4 full beats. Use steady air and hold for 4 beats.

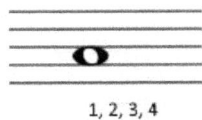

Dotted Quarter notes last for one and a half beats (that's 3 half beats).

How it works

A dot adds a little extra time—half the value of the note it's attached to.

Dotted Half notes each count for 3 beats. Use steady air and hold for 3 beats.

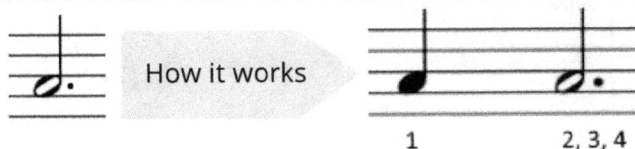

How it works

B Major Scale (Up)

This is the B major scale ascending. The scale begins on the B note and moves higher in sound with each new note. The B major scale includes the notes B, C#, D#, E, F#, G#, and A#.

For beginners, playing full scales can take time. The lower notes need more air, not tighter embouchure. And they need more practice too, and that is perfectly fine. Play the notes you can, learn them at your own pace, and grow into the rest as you continue.

Remember, each note comes with a fingering diagram showing you which keys to press.
   - Black circles mean press this key down.
   - White and Gray circles mean don't press this key.

Scan the QR Code

to Listen to the scale!

B Major Scale (Down)

Here is the B major scale descending. The scale begins on the higher B note and every new note goes lower in sound. For the B major scale descending we will play the notes B, A#, G#, F#, E, D#, C#, then back to B, only lower.

For beginners, playing full scales can take time. For many players, descending scales feel different than ascending scales. The lower notes need steady air support and a relaxed embouchure to speak clearly. Take your time and focus on keeping the sound full and even as you move downward. Play the notes you can, learn them at your own pace.

Remember, each note comes with a fingering diagram showing you which keys to press.
   - Black circles mean press this key down.
   - White and Gray circles mean don't press this key.

Scan the QR Code

to Listen to the scale!

E Major Scale (Up)

This is the E major scale ascending. The scale begins on the E note and moves higher in sound with each new note. The E major scale includes the notes E, F#, G#, A, B, C#, and D#. The written low E (E3) is the lowest note on a standard, non-extended bass clarinet. Instruments equipped with low-note extensions can play below E3, reaching as low as written C (C3).

For beginners, playing full scales can take time. The lower notes need more air, not tighter embouchure. And they need more practice too, and that is perfectly fine. Play the notes you can, learn them at your own pace, and grow into the rest as you continue.

Remember, each note comes with a fingering diagram showing you which keys to press.
- Black circles mean press this key down.
- White and Gray circles mean don't press this key.

Scan the QR Code

to Listen to the scale!

E Major Scale (Down)

Here is the E major scale descending. The scale begins on the higher E note and every new note goes lower in sound. For the E major scale descending we will play the notes E, D#, C#, B, A, G#, F#, then back to E, only lower. The written low E (E3) is the lowest note on a standard, non-extended bass clarinet. Instruments equipped with low-note extensions can play below E3, reaching as low as written C (C3).

For beginners, playing full scales can take time. For many players, descending scales feel different than ascending scales. The lower notes need steady air support and a relaxed embouchure to speak clearly. Take your time and focus on keeping the sound full and even as you move downward. Play the notes you can, learn them at your own pace.

Remember, each note comes with a fingering diagram showing you which keys to press.
- Black circles mean press this key down.
- White and Gray circles mean don't press this key.

Scan the QR Code

to Listen to the scale!

Db Major Scale (Up)

This is the Db major scale ascending. The scale begins on the Db note and moves higher in sound with each new note. The Db major scale includes the notes Db, Eb, F, Gb, Ab, Bb, and C.

For beginners, playing higher notes can take time. The upper notes need faster, focused air and steady embouchure support, not added pressure or biting. Keep the throat open and the air moving freely as you ascend. Play the notes you can at your own pace, and let the upper range develop gradually as you continue.

Remember, each note comes with a fingering diagram showing you which keys to press.
   - Black circles mean press this key down.
   - White and Gray circles mean don't press this key.

Scan the QR Code

to Listen to the scale!

D♭ Major Scale (Down)

Here is the D♭ major scale descending. The scale begins on the higher D♭ note and every new note goes lower in sound. For the D♭ major scale descending we will play the notes D♭, C, B♭, A♭, G♭, F, E♭, then back to D♭, only lower.

For beginners, playing higher notes can take time. The upper notes need faster, focused air and steady embouchure support, not added pressure or biting. Keep the throat open and the air moving freely as you descend. Play the notes you can at your own pace, and let the upper range develop gradually as you continue.

Remember, each note comes with a fingering diagram showing you which keys to press.
   - Black circles mean press this key down.
   - White and Gray circles mean don't press this key.

Scan the QR Code

to Listen to the scale!

A♭ Major Scale (Up)

This is the A♭ major scale ascending. The scale begins on the A♭ note and moves higher in sound with each new note. The A♭ major scale includes the notes A♭, B♭, C, D♭, E♭, F, and G.

For beginners, playing full scales can take time. The lower notes need more air, not tighter embouchure. And they need more practice too, and that is perfectly fine. Play the notes you can, learn them at your own pace, and grow into the rest as you continue.

Remember, each note comes with a fingering diagram showing you which keys to press.
- Black circles mean press this key down.
- White and Gray circles mean don't press this key.

Scan the QR Code

to Listen to the scale!

A♭ Major Scale (Down)

Here is the A♭ major scale descending. The scale begins on the higher A♭ note and every new note goes lower in sound. For the A♭ major scale descending we will play the notes A♭, G, F, E♭, D♭, C, B♭, then back to A♭, only lower.

For beginners, playing full scales can take time. For many players, descending scales feel different than ascending scales. The lower notes need steady air support and a relaxed embouchure to speak clearly. Take your time and focus on keeping the sound full and even as you move downward. Play the notes you can, learn them at your own pace.

Remember, each note comes with a fingering diagram showing you which keys to press.
- Black circles mean press this key down.
- White and Gray circles mean don't press this key.

Scan the QR Code to Listen to the scale!

A Major Scale (Up)

This is the A major scale ascending. The scale begins on the A note and moves higher in sound with each new note. The A major scale includes the notes A, B, C#, D, E, F#, and G#.

For beginners, playing full scales can take time. The lower notes need more air, not tighter embouchure. And they need more practice too, and that is perfectly fine. Play the notes you can, learn them at your own pace, and grow into the rest as you continue.

Remember, each note comes with a fingering diagram showing you which keys to press.
   - Black circles mean press this key down.
   - White and Gray circles mean don't press this key.

Scan the QR Code

to Listen to the scale!

A Major Scale (Down)

Here is the A major scale descending. The scale begins on the higher A note and every new note goes lower in sound. For the A major scale descending we will play the notes A, G#, F#, E, D, C#, B, then back to A, only lower.

For beginners, playing full scales can take time. For many players, descending scales feel different than ascending scales. The lower notes need steady air support and a relaxed embouchure to speak clearly. Take your time and focus on keeping the sound full and even as you move downward. Play the notes you can, learn them at your own pace.

Remember, each note comes with a fingering diagram showing you which keys to press.
- Black circles mean press this key down.
- White and Gray circles mean don't press this key.

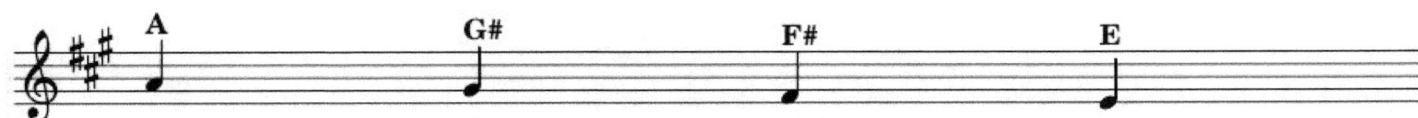

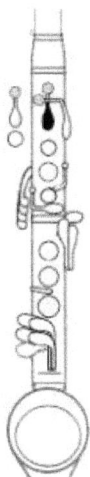

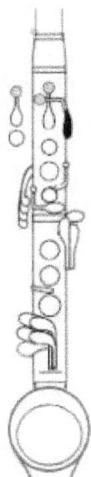

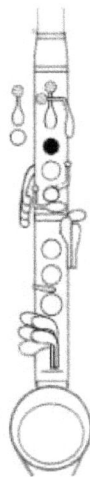

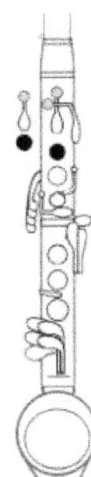

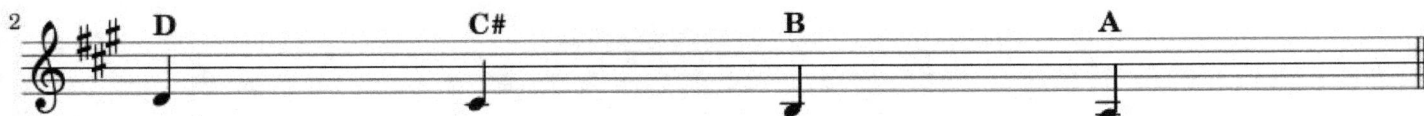

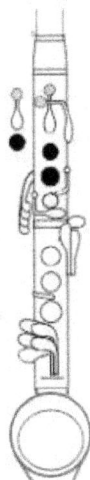

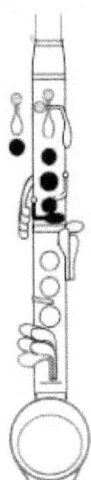

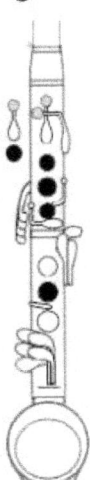

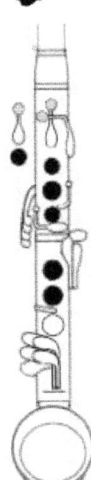

Scan the
QR Code

to Listen to
the scale!

G♭ Major Scale (Up)

This is the G♭ major scale ascending. The scale begins on the G♭ note and moves higher in sound with each new note. The G♭ major scale includes the notes G♭, A♭, B♭, C♭ (C♭ is the same as B), D♭, E♭, and F.

In music, some notes can have two different names even though they sound exactly the same. This is called being **enharmonic.** C♭ (C flat) and B are one of these pairs. When you see C♭, it means play one half step lower than C. When you move one half step lower from C, you land on B. So even though they look different on paper, C♭ and B sound the same when you play them.

Remember, each note comes with a fingering diagram showing you which keys to press.
- Black circles mean press this key down.
- White and Gray circles mean don't press this key.

Scan the QR Code

to Listen to the scale!

G♭ Major Scale (Down)

Here is the G♭ major scale descending. The scale begins on the higher G♭ note and every new note goes lower in sound. For the G♭ major scale descending we will play the notes G♭, F, E♭, D♭, C♭ (B), B♭, A♭, then back to G♭, only lower.

In music, some notes can have two different names even though they sound exactly the same. This is called being **enharmonic**. C♭ (C flat) and B are one of these pairs. When you see C♭, it means play one half step lower than C. When you move one half step lower from C, you land on B. So even though they look different on paper, C♭ and B sound the same when you play them.

Remember, each note comes with a fingering diagram showing you which keys to press.
   - Black circles mean press this key down.
   - White and Gray circles mean don't press this key.

Scan the QR Code to Listen to the scale!

Mary Had a Little Lamb

Lowell Mason (1831)

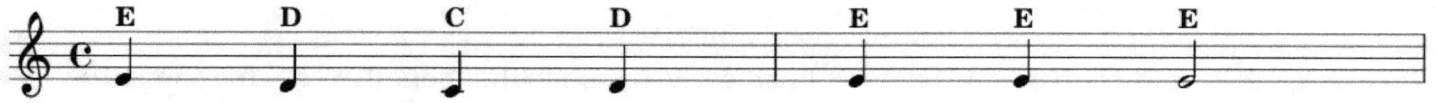

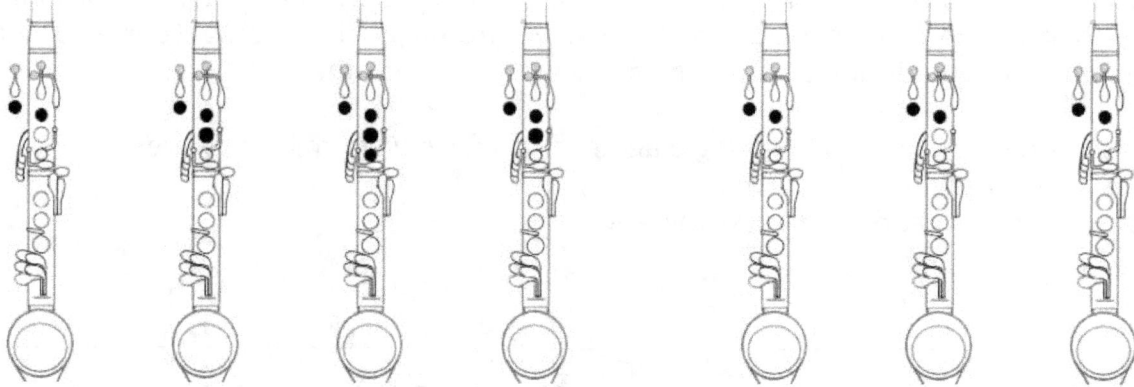

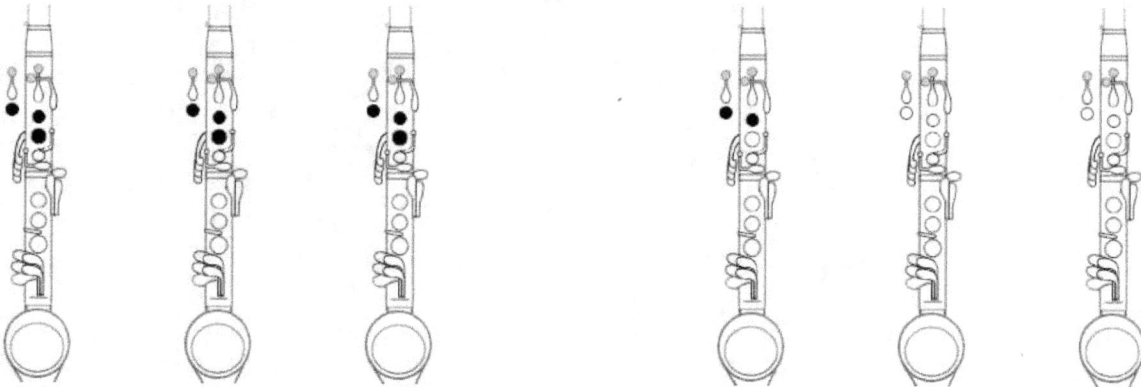

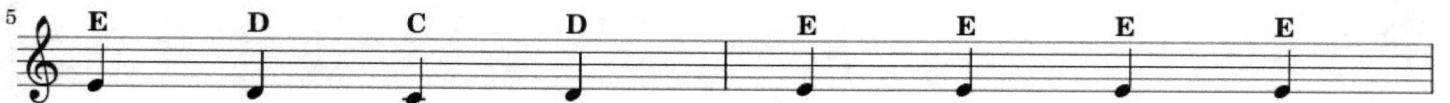

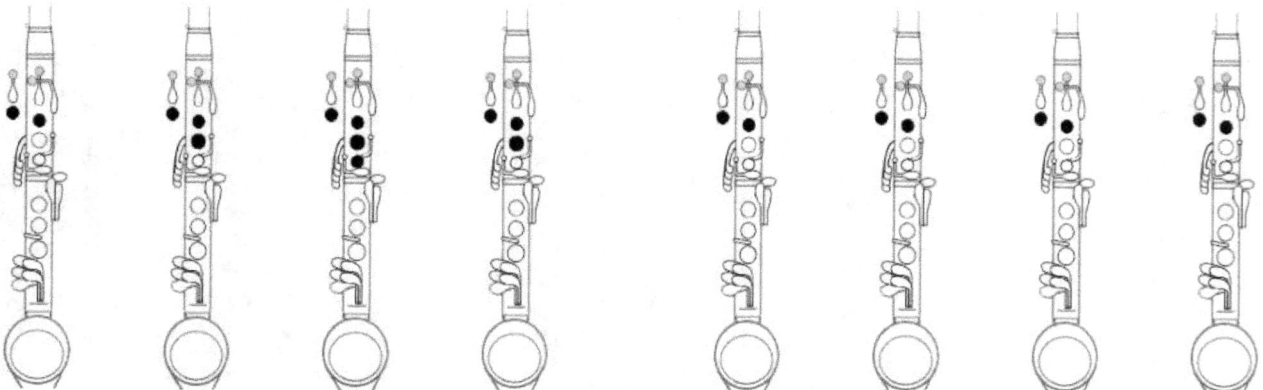

The Legend of Mary and Her Lamb

As the legend goes, this song was inspired by an actual event involving a girl named Mary Elizabeth Sawyer (1806–1889), who lived in Sterling, Massachusetts. According to Mary's writings, when she was a young girl, she nursed a sickly lamb back to health, and the lamb became attached to her. One day, the lamb followed Mary to school, creating a scene that amused her classmates and teacher.

Today, the Redstone Schoolhouse, where Mary's lamb supposedly followed her, is preserved as a historical site in Sudbury, Massachusetts, and continues to commemorate the tale.

Scan the QR Code

to Listen to the song!

Twinkle Twinkle Little Star

Traditional (1806)

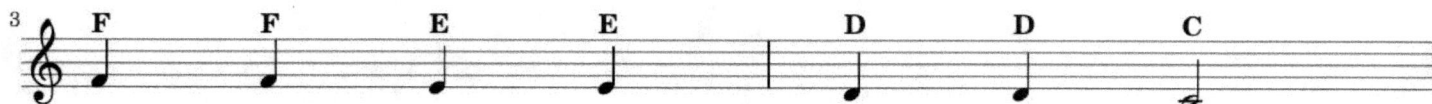

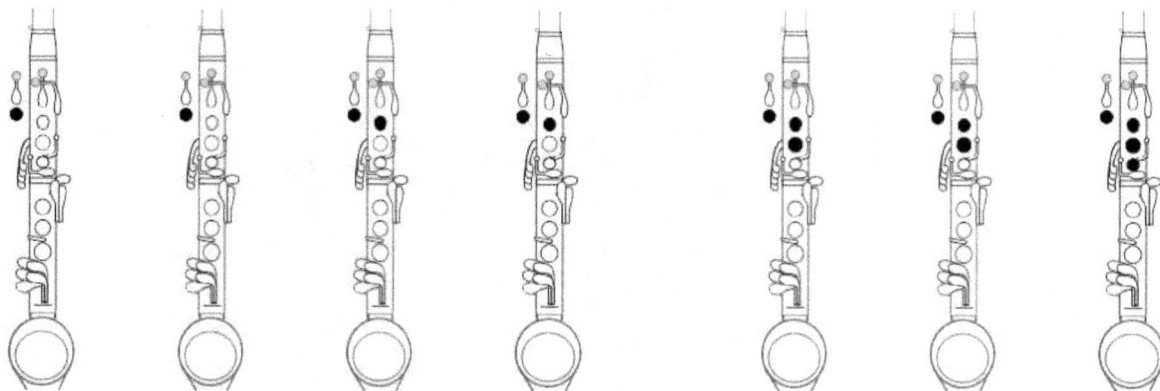

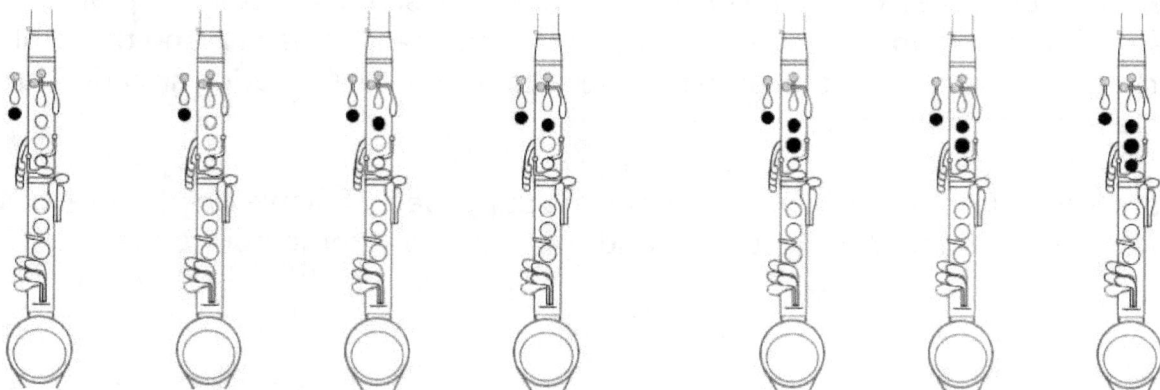

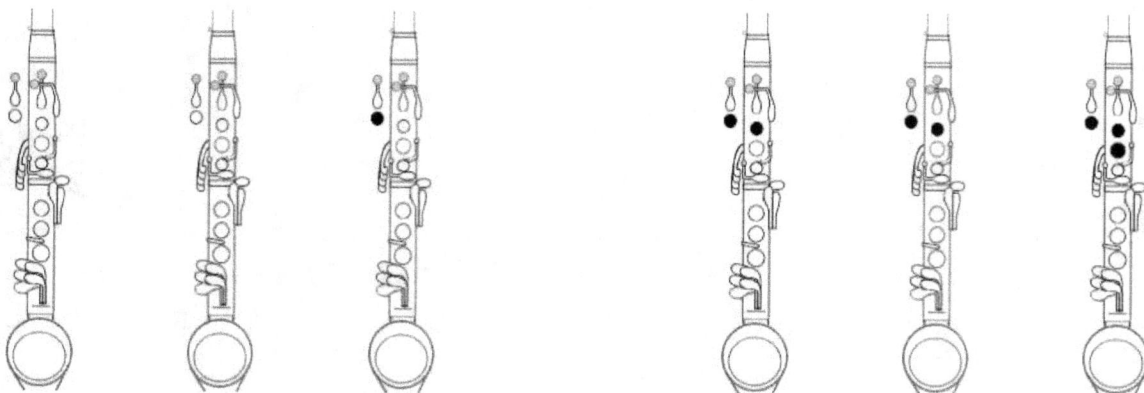

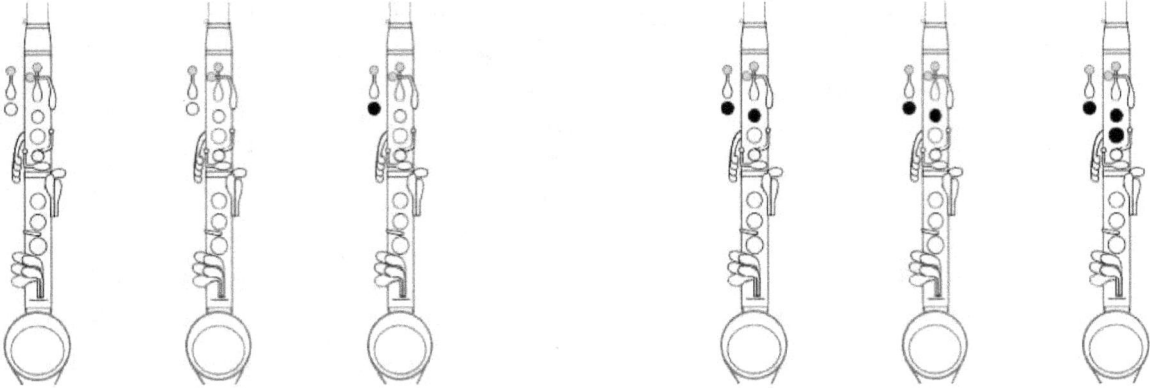

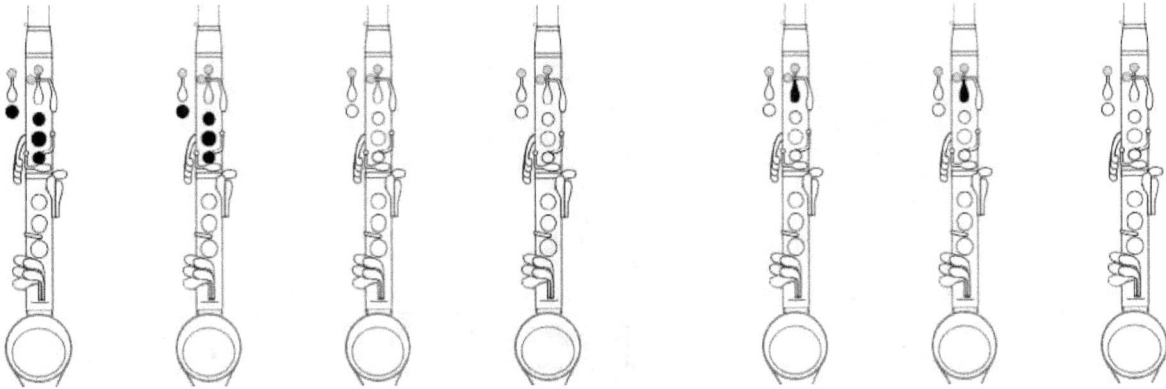

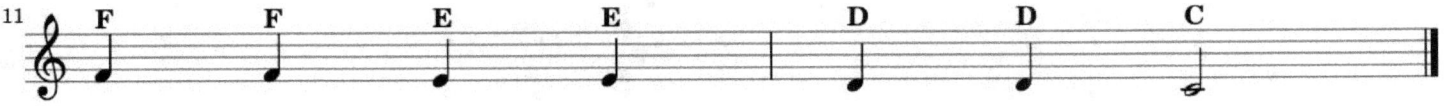

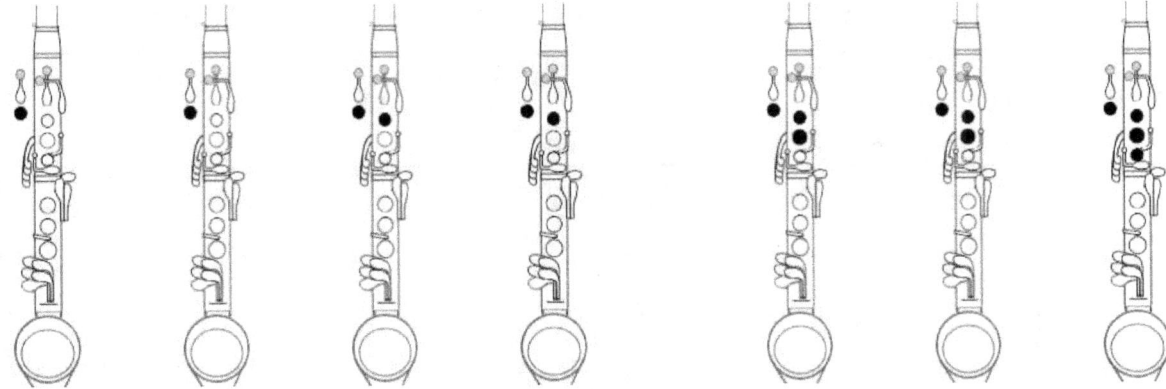

Scan the QR Code to Listen to the song!

Frère Jacques (Brother John)

Traditional French (18th Century)

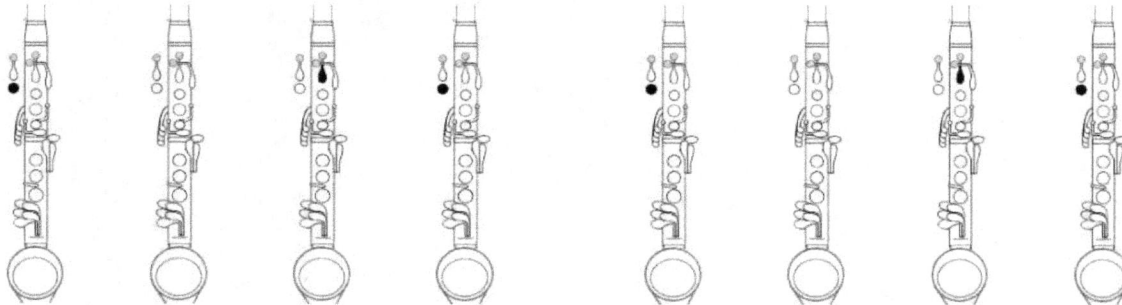

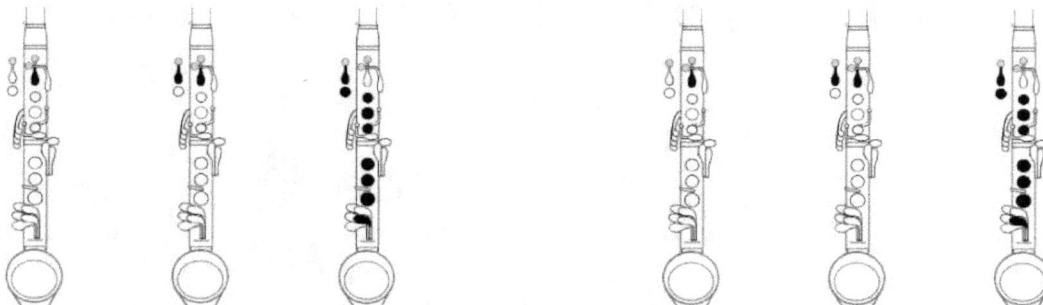

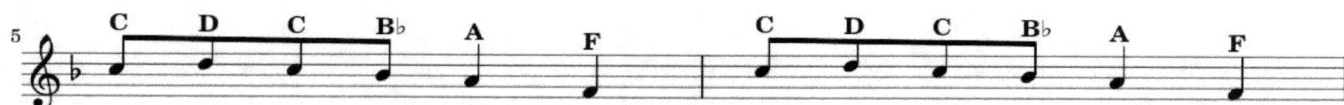

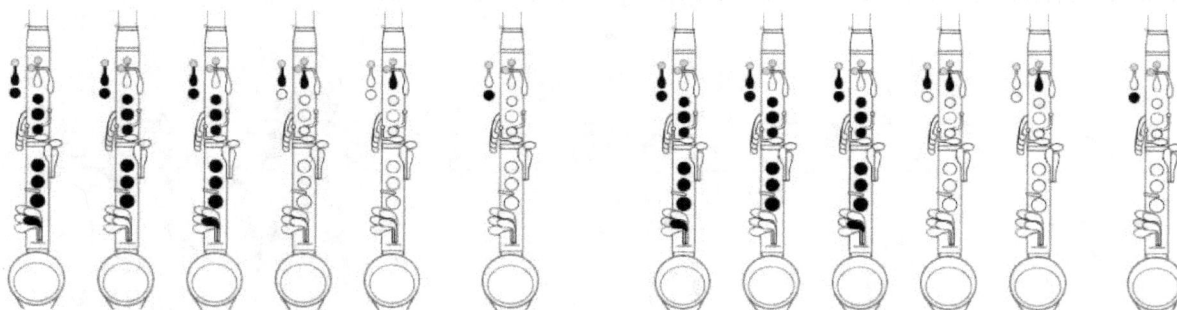

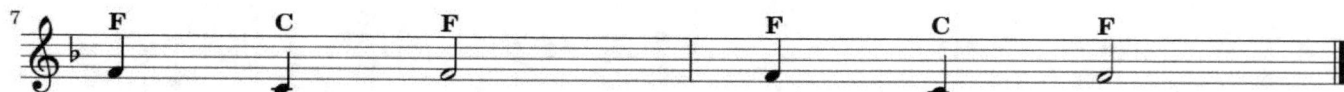

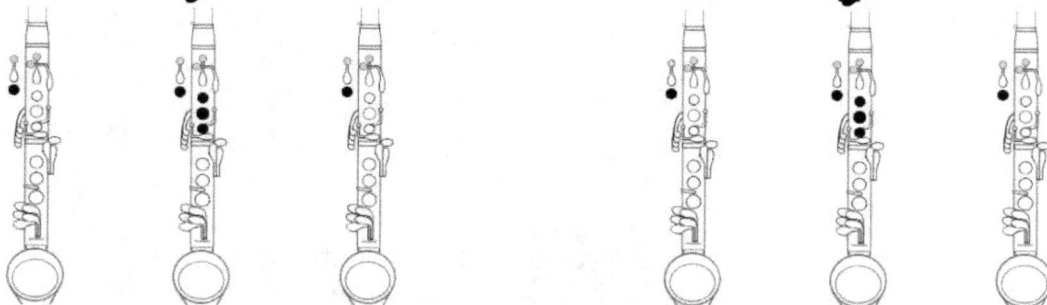

Scan the QR Code

to Listen to the song!

Pop Goes the Weasel

Traditional English (c1850)

Scan the QR Code

to Listen to the song!

Ring Around the Rosie

Traditional English (19th Century)

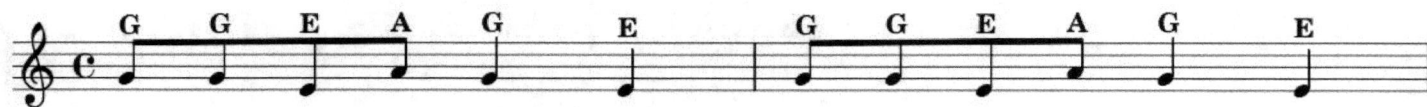

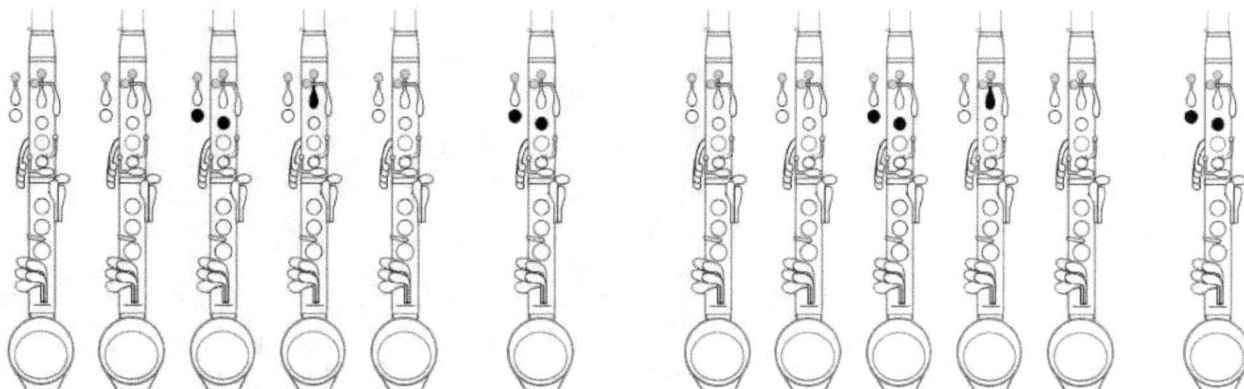

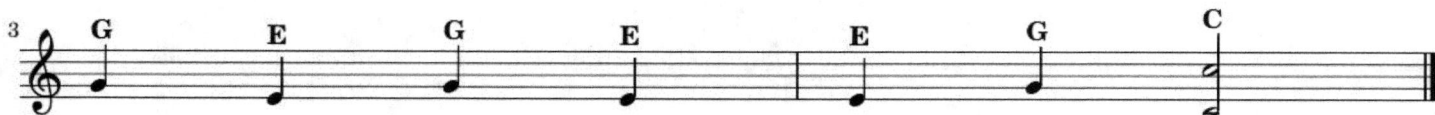

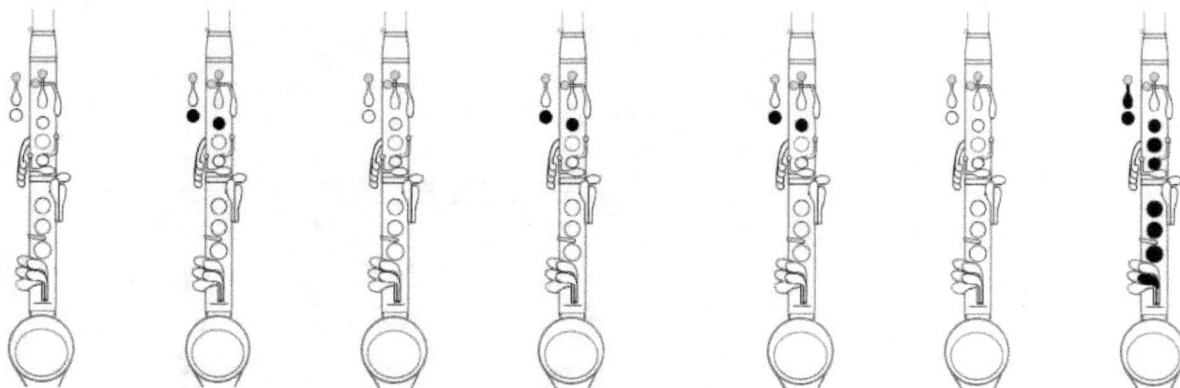

How About a Challenge?

Most of this song stays in a comfortable range using notes you already know. At the end, try the higher C5 as a challenge note. If it speaks clearly, great. If not, don't worry. Play the easier C4 instead and come back to the challenge later.

The goal is not to force the note, but to explore how the bass clarinet feels as you move higher. Take a relaxed breath, use steady air, and listen carefully to your sound.

Scan the
QR Code

to Listen to
the song!

C5 - Challenge

C4 - Standard

Row Row Row Your Boat

Traditional American (19th Century)

Scan the
QR Code

to Listen to
the song!

This Old Man

Traditional English (19th Century)

Scan the QR Code to Listen to the song!

London Bridge is Falling Down

Traditional English (18th Century)

Scan the QR Code

to Listen to the song!

It's a Jazzy Day!

Martin Freres (2025)

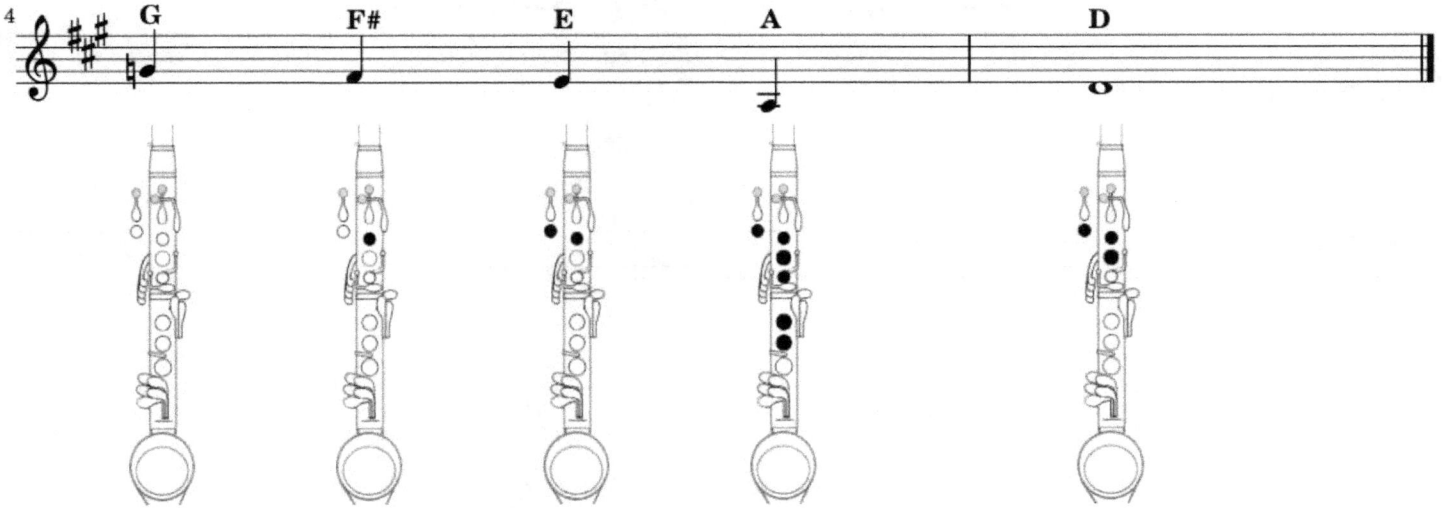

It's a Jazzy Day!

This tune plays low notes and then jumps an octave higher. An **octave** is the distance between two notes with the same letter name, where one sounds higher or lower than the other. In this song, you can hear that jump between the lower and higher A note.

IT'S A JAZZY DAY

Scan the
QR Code

to Listen to
the song!

Camptown Races

Stephen Foster (1850)

Stephen C. Foster (1826–1864)

Known as the "Father of American Music," Stephen Foster wrote songs that became part of America's cultural history. Born in Pennsylvania on July 4, 1826, he composed beloved tunes such as *Camptown Races, Oh! Susanna,* and *That's What's the Matter*, all featured in this book. His music remains timeless, simple, and memorable, ideal for learning melody, rhythm, and phrasing.

Scan the QR Code

to Listen to the song!

Oh! Susanna

Stephen Foster (1848)

Scan the QR Code to Listen to the song!

That's What's the Matter

Stephen Foster (1862)

Scan the QR Code

to Listen to the song!

Ode to Joy

Ludwig van Beethoven (1824)

Scan the QR Code to Listen to the song!

She'll Be Comin' 'Round the Mountain

Traditional American (19th Century)

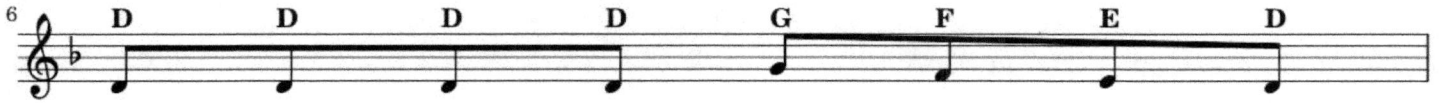

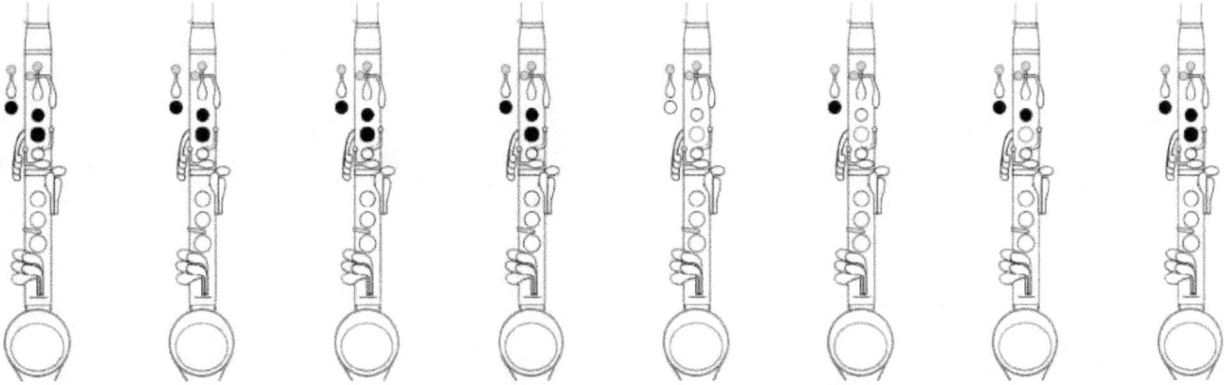

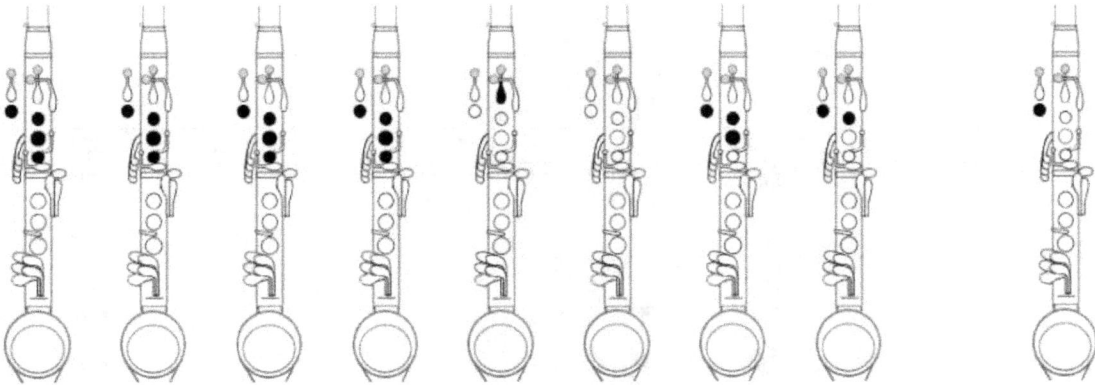

Scan the QR Code

to Listen to the song!

When the Saints Go Marching In

Traditional American (19th Century)

Scan the
QR Code

to Listen to
the song!

Amazing Grace

William Walker (1835)

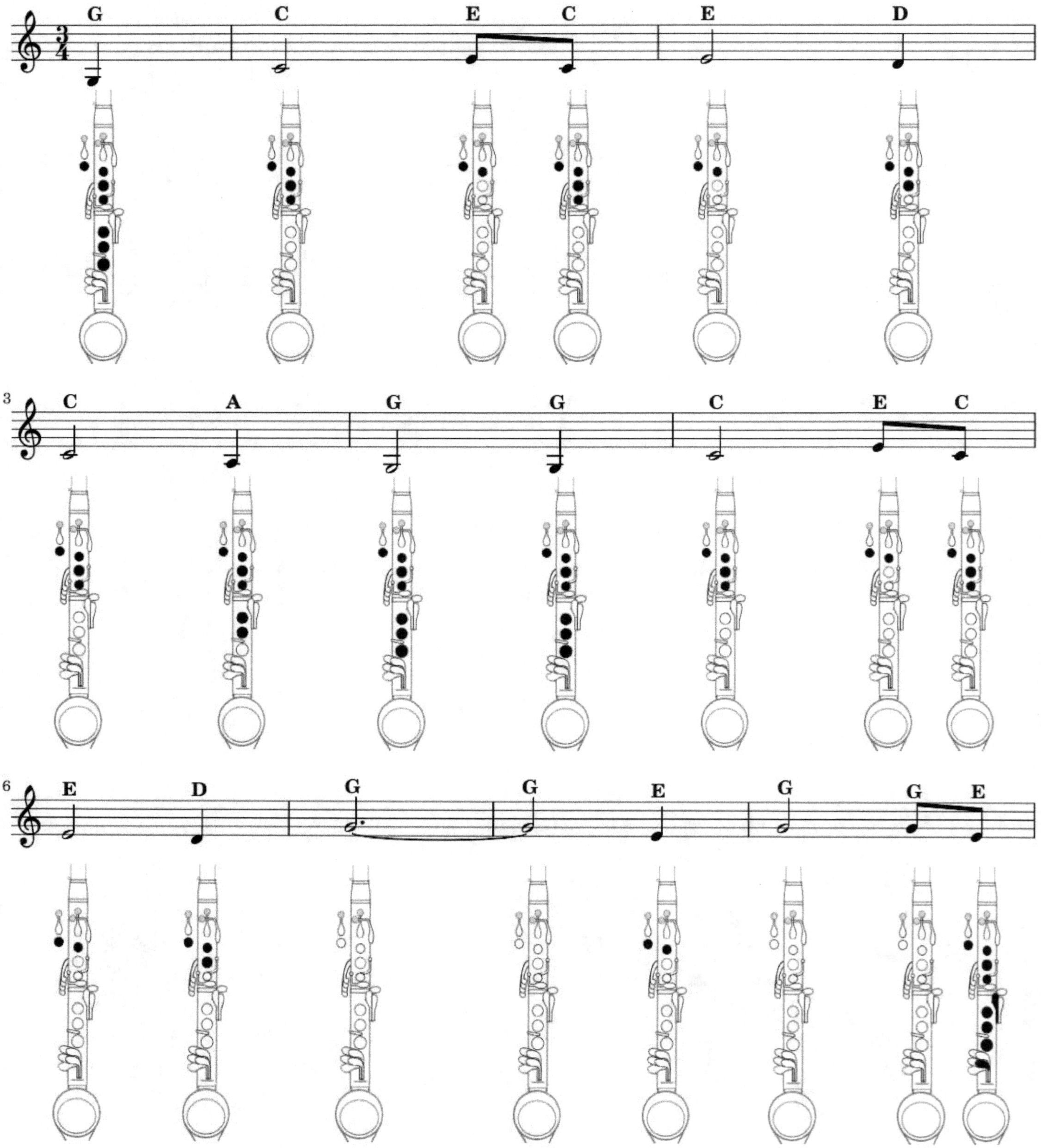

Musical History of "Amazing Grace"

The tune we use for *Amazing Grace* is an early American melody called *New Britain*. It's an old American melody that first appeared in a music book in 1829.

In 1835, a musician named William Walker arranged the *Amazing Grace* words with the *New Britain* melody in his book *Southern Harmony*. The two fit so well that the pairing quickly became popular all over the world. The rest is history!

Scan the QR Code

to Listen to the song!

Jingle Bells

J. Pierpont (1857)

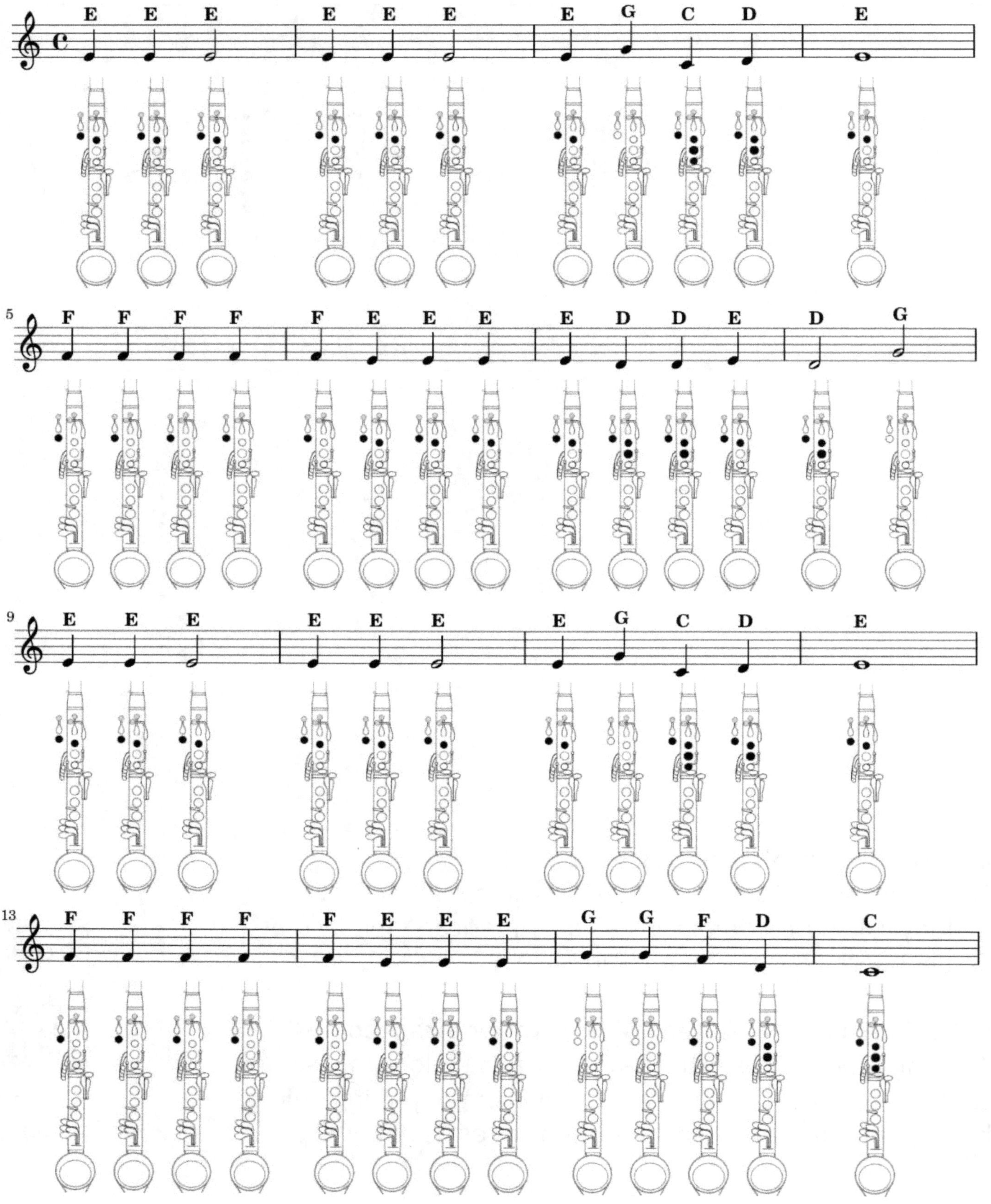

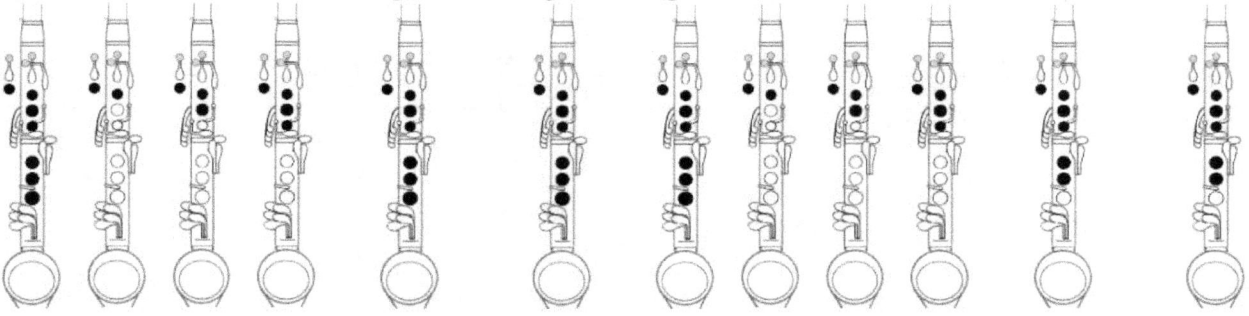

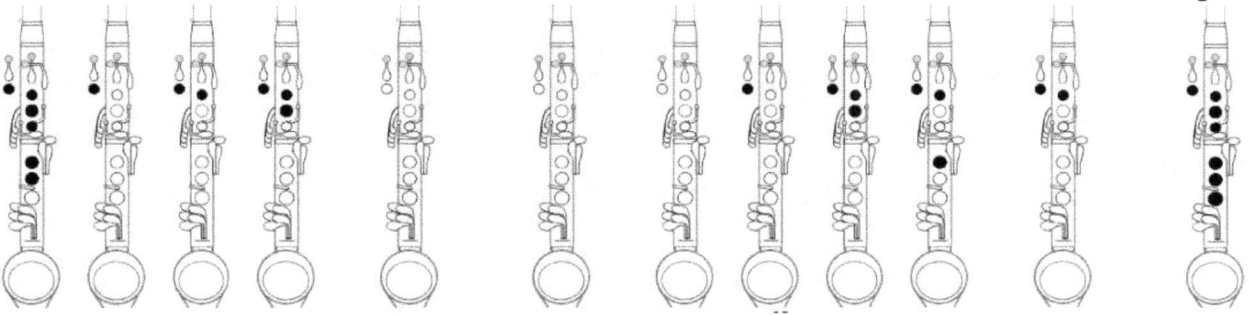

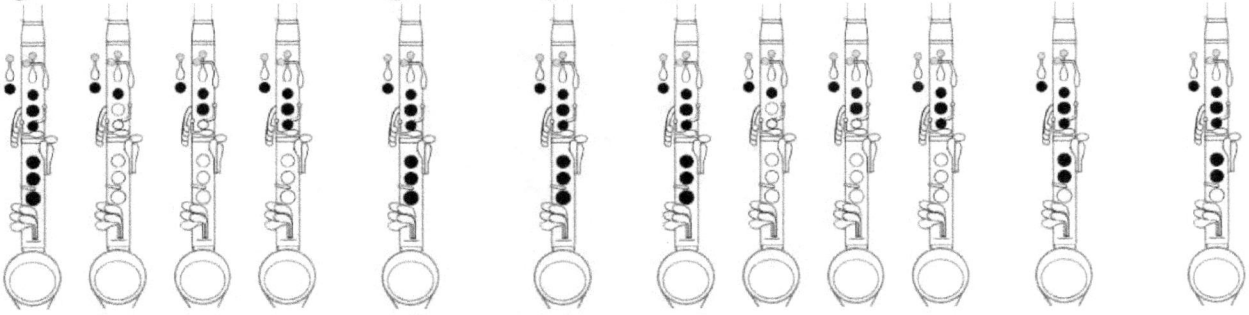

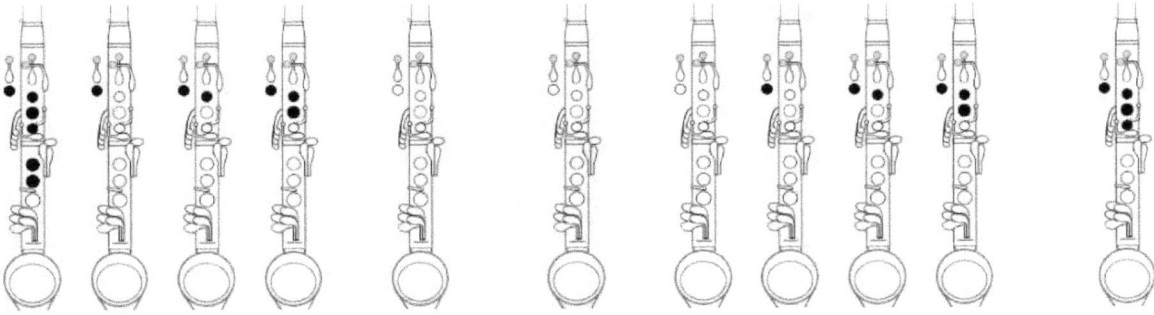

Scan the
QR Code

to Listen to
the song!

Up On the Housetop

Benjamin Hanby (1864)

Scan the QR Code to Listen to the song!

Bass Clarinet Fingering Chart

The Bass Clarinet Fingering Chart begins with the note E3. Next, the chart rises step by step, showing flats (♭) and sharps (#), all the way up to C6. This fingering chart is presented as a chromatic scale.

A **Chromatic Scale** is a musical scale that goes up or down by half steps, the smallest steps in music. Think of playing every single note in order, without skipping any. Scan the QR code to listen to the whole scale from written E3 to C6, which sounds from concert D2 up to B♭4.

E3 to D♭4

Bass Clarinet Fingering Chart

The numbers next to the notes, such as 3, 4, 5, or 6, are called octave numbers. You'll see them written with note names in this chart, like D4 or F5. **Octave numbers** show how high or low a note sounds. Each time you move to the next higher C note, you move up one octave and the number increases by one. The octave number helps identify which version of a note you are playing, whether it is in a lower, middle, or higher range on the instrument.

D4 to B4

11

D4	D#4 E♭4	E4	F4	F#4 G♭4

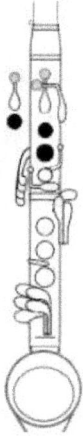 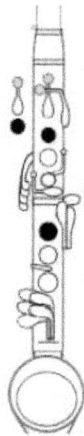 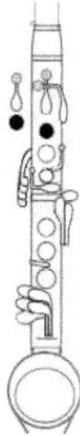  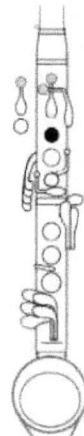

16

G4	G#4 A♭4	A4	A#4 B♭4	B4

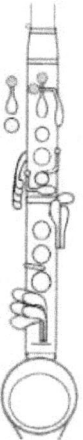 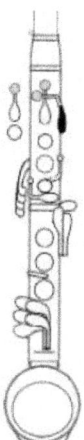 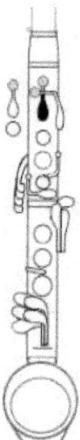 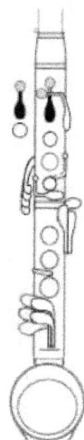 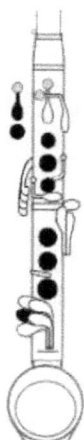

Bass Clarinet Fingering Chart

C5 to A5

Register boundaries on bass clarinet may vary by instrument and player. In this book, notes up to D5 are treated as the clarion (mid-range), while notes at and above E♭5 are treated as the altissimo (upper range) due to changes in acoustic response and voicing requirements.

21

C5	C#5 D♭5	D5	D#5 E♭5	E5

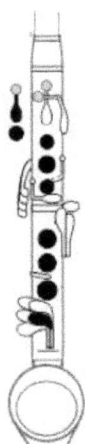 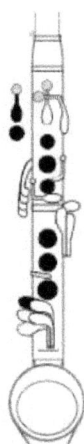 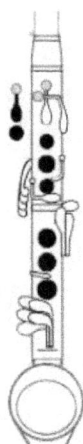 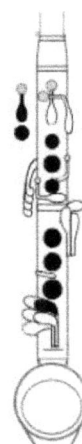 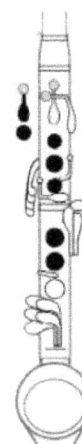

26

F5	F#5 G♭5	G5	G#5 A♭5	A5

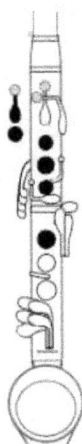 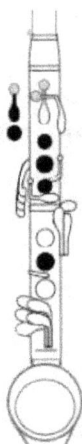 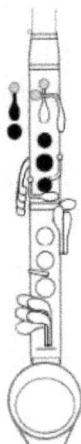  

Scan the QR Code   to Listen to the scale!

Bass Clarinet Fingering Chart

Advanced / Instrument-Dependent Range

The following fingerings may vary in response and stability depending on the instrument model, keywork, and player voicing. These notes are included as reference fingerings for advancing players. While some professional players can reach notes as high as written C7 on bass clarinet, exploration of those fingerings is beyond the scope of this book.

A#5 to C6

Bass Clarinet Registers

While descriptions of bass clarinet registers may vary across sources, register definitions developed for other clarinets do not transfer cleanly to the bass clarinet due to differences in bore size, venting, and acoustic behavior. On bass clarinet, register changes reflect how the air column vibrates, not just where notes appear on the staff. Higher notes gradually rely less on the full length of the bore and more on venting and overtone control, which is why upper registers feel and respond differently.

Boundaries may vary by instrument and player

The Note You Play is Not the Note You Hear

The bass clarinet is a B-flat instrument, often called a **transposing instrument**, which means the note written on the page is not the same as the note you hear. When a bass clarinet player reads a written C, the sound produced is a B-flat at concert pitch, and it sounds much lower than it appears on the staff. **Concert pitch** refers to the actual sound you hear rather than what is written on the music.

The piano, on the other hand, is a non-transposing instrument, so what you see is what you hear. Middle C on the music staff is the same middle C you hear when you press the key on the piano. On bass clarinet, players learn to think in two ways at once. They read the written notes and also learn how those notes sound in real life.

Let's see how the note you play is not the note you hear on a bass clarinet.

The Note Written Versus the Note Heard (Concert Pitch)

This example shows pairs of notes that represent the same sound in two different ways. In each pair, the written note on the staff for bass clarinet is shown first, followed immediately by the concert pitch that you actually hear from the instrument.

Because the bass clarinet is a B♭ instrument, *every written note* sounds lower by one octave and one whole step. For example, a written note E3 sounds as note D2, a written G4 sounds as F3, and a written B4 sounds as A3. Higher notes follow the same rule, so a written D#5 (same as E♭5) sounds as C#4 (same as D♭4).

This visual shows how the same musical pitch can be written differently depending on the instrument. Understanding this relationship helps bass clarinet players read music correctly and understand how their part fits with other instruments like the piano.

66

www.ingramcontent.com/pod-product-compliance
Lightning Source LLC
LaVergne TN
LVHW081336060426

835513LV00014B/1311